HOW
TO
MEET
SOMEONE
(NOT ONLINE)

How to Meet Someone (Not Online)

13-Digit ISBN: 978-1-64643-166-3
10-Digit ISBN: 1-64643-166-9

This book may be ordered by mail from the publisher. Please include $5.99 for postage and handling. Please support your local bookseller first!

Books published by Cider Mill Press Book Publishers are available at special discounts for bulk purchases in the United States by corporations, institutions, and other organizations. For more information, please contact the publisher.

Cider Mill Press Book Publishers
"Where good books are ready for press"
PO Box 454
12 Spring Street
Kennebunkport, Maine 04046

Visit us online!
cidermillpress.com

Typography: Brandon Grotesque

Printed in China
1 2 3 4 5 6 7 8 9 0
First Edition

HOW TO MEET SOMEONE
(NOT ONLINE)

**EVERYTHING YOU NEED
TO FIND LOVE AND CREATE
MEANINGFUL RELATIONSHIPS
IN THE DIGITAL AGE**

by Sharon Gilchrest O'Neill, Ed.S.

CIDER MILL
PRESS

BOOK
PUBLISHERS
KENNEBUNKPORT, MAINE

HOW TO MEET SOMEONE (NOT ONLINE)

IS FOR EVERYONE WANTING TO MEET PEOPLE IN THE REAL WORLD:

WHETHER YOU ARE
LOOKING FOR A FRIEND
OR A PARTNER; WHETHER
YOU HAVE JUST SET OUT
INTO THE WORLD ON
YOUR OWN; OR HAVE
LIVED LONG ENOUGH
TO HAVE EXPERIENCED
THE DEATH OF FRIENDS
OR PARTNERS. OR MAYBE
YOU HAVE GIVEN UP
AFTER A LONG AND
DIFFICULT EXPERIENCE
WITH A PARTNER OR
FRIEND, OR HAVE GONE
THROUGH A DIVORCE.

THIS BOOK WAS WRITTEN TO MOTIVATE YOU AND GIVE YOU A NEW PERSPECTIVE.

READ ON TO GAIN THE KNOWLEDGE AND SKILLS FOR MEETING SOMEONE IN THE REAL WORLD.

INTRO-DUCTION

How to Meet Someone (Not Online) is an invitation, maybe even a challenge, to consider the allegedly outmoded notion of actually meeting people in-person. Face-to-face. In the real world.

For some time now, we have been led to believe that the online world is the best for just about everything in our lives. It helps us manage money and pay bills, shop, read, work remotely, and much more. Most of us would agree that we greatly appreciate the online world for the many mundane and complex tasks that it handles to make our lives easier. Most would also agree that we certainly hope we never have to take back any of those tasks. But do we really continue to believe that the online world is best for meeting people? For finding a good friend, or a possible lifelong partner?

Since the launch of commercial sites for meeting people over two decades ago, surveys have shown that users are feeling increasingly frustrated rather than hopeful. There are concerns about safety, scams, harassment, and the common occurrence of the lies that people tell to appear more desirable, more attractive. Unfortunately, dishonesty is as easy as it is pervasive online.

There is constant swiping and scrolling and texting that too often goes nowhere. We are continually checking our progress and hoping. We struggle with how much or how little to tell about ourselves. We wonder what is happening to our efforts at the other end. We spend countless hours composing the perfect texts only to be ghosted. I wonder, are there actually perfect text messages in the quest of getting to know someone online? We persevere again and again, without satisfaction.

Trying to meet people online is not working. Surveys show that only a small share of the adult population across the United States has found a significant relationship through meeting online. The process is often described as superficial, one-dimensional, and lacking the ability to assess compatibility.

So, let's take Albert Einstein's words to heart, doing the same thing over and over again and expecting different results is insanity. Allow yourself to imagine the feeling of freedom in face-to-face conversations, rather than trying to keep on communicating in a less than real world. We can do better, much better, once we decide to come out from behind our computers and phones.

LET ME BEGIN WITH A STORY

She was late leaving her office on the way to class, and therefore anxious, hating to have all eyes on her as she opened the classroom door to a room filled with weary students—the first night of the last class in her degree program. The professor pointed to the only vacant chair in the very back corner of the room. She made her way down the aisle piled high with book bags, briefcases, and warm winter jackets, including a beautiful cream color fur coat that she very carefully began to step over. But instead, she almost fell over it with a scream, as a tall, long-haired dog (not a coat) stood up! So much for not wanting all eyes on her. She watched the dog and its owner throughout the class and found them quite interesting. She promised herself that she would say hello and introduce herself to the both of them at the next class meeting. She wasn't quite ready to do so immediately that evening.

Well, that was many years ago when she followed up and met a most fascinating and attractive guy who would become her husband five years later. They would always be grateful for Babe, the gorgeous Afghan Hound, who provided the opportunity for their fortuitous meeting!

Now, wouldn't it be wonderful to find our friends and partners just as easily! We fantasize and imagine how it will all happen. We dream it, and some of us meet with psychics, palm readers, and astrologers to learn how the stars and planets influence our lives. Or we might believe in destiny, that one's soul mate or best friend will eventually or suddenly come into our life. So we wait. We wish when we blow out our birthday candles. We say we are eager for the real thing, but instead, we play a game of pretend online.

We may also hold to the theory that there is one perfect person for each of us and that the stars will eventually align. We are asking quite a lot from the universe. It is easy to see how we gravitated toward meeting people through technology, but that process is not living up to its promises.

Meeting people is one of our most important tasks in life, one we need to take back. Too much is missed online that cannot be programmed into a computer. Let's take a look at what that means, and what exactly is missing.

THE HELPFUL SCIENCE FOR MEETING SOMEONE

WE WILL BEGIN WITH THE SCIENCE OF KINESICS, WHICH ADDRESSES NONVERBAL COMMUNICATIONS.

When we first meet somebody, it is initially all about the face, more specifically the expressiveness of our face. Given the 43 muscles around our eyes, nose, mouth, jaw, chin, and brow, humans are capable of thousands of expressions. The better we get to know a person, the more we understand their emotions and the feelings being conveyed. Your face is quite a dynamic instrument of communication, showing such traits as trustworthiness and sincerity. And it does not present itself well in the online world. This is compounded by our brain's ability to subconsciously process the physical cues that do not permeate the barrier of our screens.

Kinesics also shows that to establish a deeper connection with someone, the most effective and ultimately satisfying behavior one can engage in is making eye contact. Of course, you say, but eye contact can get a bit tricky. There is a "Goldilocks" amount, not too much, not too little. We've all had an experience with a person who barely makes eye contact and leaves you feeling that they were disinterested in you or in what you were saying, or both. At the other end of the spectrum, you have probably experienced someone who persistently makes eye contact. You would have loved to think that they found you enormously interesting, but the conversation quickly became uncomfortable, tiring, and perhaps off-putting.

The findings of kinesics can help us be our best natural selves.

THINK OF YOUR EYE CONTACT AS A FIRST STEP.

The best moment to make eye contact is before you begin talking with someone. The longer you wait to do so, the more difficult it becomes and the more awkward it feels. And your attention and focus, not surprisingly, will be disrupted. What should feel pleasant and gratifying, isn't. Studies suggest that we follow what is called the 50/70 rule, which means: maintaining eye contact 50% of the time when speaking and 70% when listening, and most importantly holding the contact for about four to five seconds at a time, no longer. Four or five seconds was found to be just enough time to notice the color of a person's eyes. Then slowly look away from the eyes and move your gaze around other parts of the face and then back again to the eyes. Always slowly back and forth. Never look down or away from the person as you talk. And keep in mind that it also helps if you can be in a position for your body to be facing the other person.

THIS MAY ALL SOUND OVERLY COMPLICATED, BUT YOU ARE LIKELY DOING MUCH OF IT UNCONSCIOUSLY.

And given that we can all improve our conversational abilities, you will benefit by becoming a little more aware through checking yourself from time to time. It is well worth the effort. Having a good conversation is a particularly reliable behavior that increases our happiness and puts us in a good mood.

There is also the science of proxemics to guide us regarding the appropriate amount of space between two people in conversation. Just as the amount of eye contact can interfere with having a positive discussion, so too if one's personal space is not respected (most of us have experienced that kind of discomfort while riding in an elevator). To help us put proper spacing into perspective, studies have determined these norms: for casual acquaintances and coworkers, three plus feet is acceptable; for strangers more than four feet is required; and with good friends and family it is one and a half to three feet.

It is interesting to note that these personal spatial boundaries, like eye contact, differ based on where in the world you are. For example, if you grew up in Japan, you would learn it was rude and disrespectful to make eye contact at all. And if you were raised in Argentina, you need less personal space than anyone, anywhere else in the world!

Unfortunately, sitting home alone staring at a screen has, no doubt, caused our social skills to slowly atrophy. When these skills become dormant, you cannot expect to so easily smile, say hello to a stranger, and initiate a comfortable conversation.

Which brings us to a related and well researched topic: introversion and extroversion. For a long time, the United States has been viewed as a society dominated by extroverts, people who are outgoing and overtly expressive. We tend to see people as extremes on a continuum, with the shy and reticent introverts at the far end, preferring to listen intently and talk less. Meanwhile it seemed that extroverts were everywhere: being assertive, running businesses, and loving to talk and be the ultimate host.

Some of you might even have memories of being told as a child that you were too shy and needed to come out of your shell. That you should talk more. That you should to be more like your younger sister or your best friend. Essentially, being told to become more of an extrovert. Maybe it was also implied that you would not become successful if you stayed in that shell.

Well, read on, many of you will feel vindicated! Studies now show that at least one-third of us are introverts. And over the last decade there have been well documented and exciting new insights about the advantages of being an introvert. For too long, introverts were simply defined as shy, reserved, and timid people, but no longer. Introverts are much more complex and often not shy at all. Rather, they possess a quieter power, and enjoy their solitude and time for introspection. The research is clear, introverts have been given equal recognition and acclaim, and should not be discounted because they are not extroverts.

Instead, we should all become more confident in our natural predispositions and tendencies. It is okay to prefer more solitude and small celebrations. And it is okay to prefer more social gatherings and lots of talk. But it is sometimes important to be prepared to stretch yourself beyond your normal comfort level, especially when there are important life situations to attend to or personal goals you desire to achieve. The introverts may need to be part of yet another gathering they would prefer to miss. The extrovert parent may need to let his or her child do most of the talking at bedtime.

Remember that first story I told you about the beautiful Afghan Hound? That was my personal story. It was something that was not easy for me, and I needed to "stretch" myself as you will, too, at times.

Now let's take a look at what has been learned about "opposites" attracting, whether with friends or partners. It is very common to be drawn to another person because of differences. It is interesting and fun to engage with a person unlike yourself, and to watch and admire qualities that are so different from yours. Some "opposites" do go on to have wonderful relationships, but you need to be aware of one caveat: although there are differences you may love and enjoy, for a longer, more stable relationship it is very advantageous to be in agreement concerning core values such as honesty, respect, dependability, and loyalty. Without such agreement on values, this type of relationship can become volatile with partners or friends who are too often fundamentally at odds with each other. For those who know themselves well (we'll look at that next), they will make the right decision not to persevere in the relationship, hoping that the other person will change. They will end the relationship.

Most frequently, however, and not surprisingly, we see "likes" attracting. There is less friction, less disagreement, and more satisfaction and stability.

From the start, "likes" are in agreement concerning core values; it is part of the attraction. The relationship feels safe and sound.

MORE OFTEN THESE
"LIKE" PARTNERS
SUFFER LESS
ENDINGS AND
CONTINUE ON TO
BECOME PARTNERS
IN MARRIAGE.

And as well, "like" friends become lifelong friends. Here, again, our brains figure these things out better (although, not flawlessly) in-person than online.

YOUR
TRUE SELF

IN PREPARING TO GET OUT FROM BEHIND YOUR SCREEN AND INTO THE REAL WORLD, YOU WANT TO BE ABLE TO PUT YOUR TRUE SELF OUT THERE.

So what is one's true self? It is defined as: your genuine, reliable, original, and trust-worthy self, the authentic self, the real you.

It makes sense that in trying to meet others in the online world, you have prof-fered different versions of yourself to align with varied perceived situations, whether consciously or not. It might have seemed like fun at times to see a different you in your texts, but chances are—and understandably so—that the online world may have left you confused about your true self.

Consequently, as you take on meeting people in-person *first*, it is time to stop and check in on your true self; having the capacity for developing solid relationships counts on the real you showing up. And doing well in-person is fundamentally predicated on knowing yourself as thoroughly as possible.

Some of you may have been in therapy or had a friend who helped you to become more aware of your true self. But we can all do much on our own if we are committed to learning and have an exercise to guide us. The goal here is to have an honest conversation with yourself by answering a series of questions that will uncover information, remind you of important life experiences and events, and inspire self-reflection.

IT IS MEANT
TO BE THOUGHT-
PROVOKING
THROUGH THE
TRYING ON OF NEW
IDEAS TO SEE HOW
THEY FEEL AND
WHAT MIGHT FIT,
OR NOT, INTO
YOUR TRUE SELF.

People have found that this questioning
process helps them to understand their
strengths and weaknesses, and to make
better decisions in life, and thus lessen
their inner conflicts about the actual life
they are living. In this busy world of ours,
we too easily become disconnected from
our thoughts and feelings, and can lose

track of who we really are over long periods in our life.

Those of you who have had experience with this exercise may have saved a journal or other materials that would be helpful to review. Still, I would urge you to go through the exercise again. For others this will be a new experience. In either case, having made the decision to read this book suggests there couldn't be a better time for this effort. You are definitely motivated.

HOW TO BEGIN?

Set aside some time in a quiet room, where you will not be interrupted. Don't expect to complete the process in one sitting. This is not a questionnaire with multiple choice answers. I suggest that you first capture in writing your initial responses in a journal.

Find a journal you love and will always keep.

Don't lose those first thoughts that burst forth from your mind. Don't overthink. You will go back again at a later time to increase the depth of your thinking and responses. You might also have your own related questions to add to the list. Just go with your thoughts. Get it all down on paper in any way you like. Words, sentences, paragraphs, lists, sketches, your stream of consciousness, whatever works for you.

The 15 questions do not have to be taken in any particular order. Some people prefer focusing on one question at a time over the course of a week or month. And certainly, there are no right or wrong answers. You might find it helpful to read each question as if a close friend or therapist was asking it, and you are pouring your heart out to that person. You want to be understood, and you want to give all the details. In doing so, you will keep increasing your self-awareness. Resist the temptation to edit.

Some people find it helpful, when doing their assessment, to look at photos, cards, or other memorabilia that they have saved over the years. This assessment process can become powerful material that helps guide you in staying the course in some areas of your life and making changes with actionable ideas in other areas. Your true self will feel more comfortable in considering new paths and making decisions.

STAY CURIOUS.
KEEP ADDING
MORE TO YOUR
RESPONSES.
BE SKEPTICAL.
BE TOUGH ON
YOURSELF.
DEBATE.
PROBE. DOUBT.
REEXAMINE.
INTERROGATE
YOURSELF.
BEFRIEND
YOURSELF.

PERSONAL ASSESSMENT AND SELF-DISCOVERY QUESTIONS:

1. How would several people close to you describe your personality?

2. How do you describe your personality? What might you like to change?

3. How were you raised?

4. How do you tell others your life story?

5. How do you describe yourself? What might you like to change?

6. What is your top priority in life right now?

7. What are you doing to achieve your top priority? Does it involve others?

8. What are your future goals and dreams? Small ones? Big ones?

9. What are your strengths, talents, and accomplishments?

10. What is a perfect day for you?

11. What are you grateful for?

12. What concerns do you have? For yourself, for others?

13. How would you describe what friendship means to you?

14. What about you makes you a good friend? A good partner? What can you do better?

15. How do you want to see yourself in one year, five years, ten years? How will you get there?

LET ME SHARE ANOTHER STORY, THIS ONE ABOUT FIRST IMPRESSIONS, ABOUT BEING YOUR TRUE SELF:

I had been working with a client for a while, sorting out the causes of her relationships falling apart, or often barely getting started. She had a career in the corporate world, was smart, interesting, and attractive with beautiful blonde hair. She always came to our sessions right after work, and looked well dressed in a business casual way, with barely a hint of makeup. We had an appointment coming up and she called to say: "I don't want to miss my session tomorrow night, but I'm meeting a new guy, some friends thought that we should get together, and I wanted to make sure I was your last client, as usual." And she continued on to explain: "Unless you have to leave your office right away, I would like to use the bathroom in your office to get changed out of my work clothes." I told her it was fine, that I needed to do some paperwork, so she could take what time she needed and it would not be an imposition.

That evening, after our session, she went into the bathroom and didn't come out for well over a half-hour. She leaned her head into my office to say good-bye and I was stunned! I took a serious double-take. She honestly looked like a different person. I couldn't believe how she had transformed herself into an overtly sexy woman. Perfectly made-up and with a dress that many would save for a more formal event. I asked where she was meeting this new guy, and it was a nice restaurant that I knew, but it was a place where she could go dressed in jeans and a pretty blouse or sweater. I wished her well. Our next session was two weeks later and discussing that dinner meeting became our work that evening.

As she explained:

They had a nice conversation, they ate a nice meal, and he said he had enjoyed meeting her.

But she doubted he would ever call again—which was true, and was often her experience.

Having seen her transformation that night I asked about her state of mind.

Did she feel comfortable? (No.)

Was she anxious throughout the dinner? (Yes.)

Was he someone she would have liked to learn more about and see again? (Yes.)

Was she pleased with how she dressed that night, the perfection of her hair and make-up, and a sexy dress? (No.)

By the end of the session she summed up what she was just beginning to understand about herself with these words: "I never think my real self will do the job!"

There is an important lesson to be learned here. For a potential partner who was *not attracted* to my client's "transformed self," there would be the usual quick disengagement, without the chance for her true self to have become known. And a potential partner who found himself *attracted* to my client's "transformed self," would eventually lose interest when her true self became evident.

We all certainly want to make good first impressions, but don't sabotage yourself. Believe in yourself.

BE YOU. JUST YOU!
IT IS ALL THAT YOU
NEED. ANYTHING
MORE IS TOO
MUCH. OUR BEST
FIRST IMPRESSION
IS ALWAYS OUR
COMFORTABLE,
TRUE SELF.

"BE WHO YOU ARE AND SAY WHAT YOU FEEL, BECAUSE THOSE WHO MIND DON'T MATTER, AND THOSE WHO MATTER DON'T MIND."

—Bernard M. Baruch

MOVE AWAY FROM THE SCREEN

NOW THAT YOU HAVE KNOWLEDGE OF THE SCIENCE OF RELATIONSHIPS AND HAVE BEGUN YOUR PERSONAL SELF-ASSESSMENT, IT IS TIME TO GET OUT FROM BEHIND YOUR COMPUTER, PUT DOWN YOUR PHONE, AND VENTURE INTO THE WORLD BEYOND.

And what do you do when you get out there? Most importantly, be yourself. It might help you to consider the two words, **"be myself,"** to be your mantra. Silently repeating a mantra will calm you. It will keep you focused and keep your mind from wandering. Mantras are a practical tool to help your concentration and for getting you in the right frame of mind. Anytime, anywhere, for any purpose. Many find that using a mantra can boost awareness of staying in the present moment, the here and now, rather than thinking about the past or future—something we definitely want for the goal of meeting someone.

Do not rush into anything. Take in the situation around you. Let's say you've walked into a park and have sat down on the last empty bench in a grouping around a duck pond. Your first inclination might be to take out your phone and settle back—that conditioned sense of not wanting to be alone (or of missing things), which ironically makes us feel more alone. Don't do it. Resist the temptation. Simply look around, relax, and take in the view.

AND THEN DO A LITTLE PRACTICING. TRY OUT SOME "WHAT IF'S" IN YOUR MIND:

Maybe you walk over to watch the ducks and there are several other people talking about whether or not you are allowed to feed the ducks. Take a few steps closer, maybe you know the answer, or could ask "Do you mind if I join in on your discussion, I was also wondering if feeding the ducks is allowed?"

What if there was a person sitting on the next bench over who was reading a book of interest to you, how might you say hello and start a conversation by asking a few questions about the book? Maybe a simple "How are you liking it, so far?"

Maybe you are someone who is thinking it has been long enough since my break-up and I am ready to get out there again. You've been watching an appealing jogger, who is now slowing down, and you ask "How was your run?"

Maybe you've noticed an older person, like yourself, who might also live alone and would enjoy a little more company. You might ask a simple question such as, "Do you also live in this area of town? I love that it is so easy to walk to this beautiful park."

BE WILLING TO MAKE THE FIRST MOVE, TO PUT YOURSELF OUT THERE.

No situation for meeting people is ever the same, so you need to be flexible; envision examples of how you can start up conversations and introduce yourself in ways that are comfortable for you. Be genuine and direct in a friendly manner, no need to come up with clever or flirty opening words. Rather, become curious. Have some expectations, but be prepared to let any of them go, and see what happens.

Honestly, what is the worst that can happen? This question may be cliché, but it is helpful to consider when determining: do the social risks of meeting a person outweigh the potential possibilities? I think you will come to a conclusion that there is little real risk.

If you are beginning to think how much easier this all felt online, it is because your ability for meeting and conversing face-to-face has been getting compromised for some time behind your screen. Those skills that we have talked about have become dormant. But before you know it, with a little practice, you will become much more confident. And keep in mind that *we all* have to go beyond our comfort zones at times.

Over the years in my work, I have seen how important it is to become a good conversationalist (talking) and a good communicator (sharing information). These skills are truly a requirement for any enjoyable and successful relationship. It is no wonder that communication and conversation issues are always at the top of the lists of reasons why people are unhappy in relationships and why they end them.

SO, WHEN STARTING OUT, TRY NOTHING MORE THAN A SMILE, OR A SIMPLE HELLO.

Make it a new habit for a while. See how that feels before you begin initiating conversations. Studies show that a smile begets feelings of happiness for both the initiator and the receiver. There is power in simple connections, even with strangers. Meeting new and different people gives you perspective on your life and empathy for others. All good stuff.

And let us not forget that there is the possibility that someone might approach *you*, so be approachable! Keep an open mind. Don't overthink. Be ready to connect and make eye contact. And do not be glued to your phone. Who knows what you might miss out on.

ALL THE PLACES YOU WILL GO

WE HAVE TALKED ABOUT SOME OF THE MORE DIFFICULT MEETINGS IN REAL LIFE: THE UNSTRUCTURED ONES.

But as the following list shows, there is an abundance of structured formats in which people get to know each other. All kinds of people assembled in all kinds of groups that you might choose to try. Start within your comfort zone: the obvious, the local places. Then over time, as your comfort level builds, take on something new. Head to a neighboring town. Join the next cooking class. Sign up for a course in the fall semester. Check out a gym. The possibilities are limitless.

BUT NOW THAT YOU
HAVE COME TO
UNDERSTAND MORE
ABOUT YOUR TRUE
SELF, CONSIDER IN
WHICH WAYS YOU
WOULD MOST ENJOY
MEETING PEOPLE.

Where do you believe you could likely find
a good friend, a good partner? Where would
you look for someone like yourself? What
would they be doing that you like doing? And
what new activity choices and places might
you want to consider?

THE POSSIBILITIES

1. **FRIENDS AND FRIENDS OF FRIENDS**

   Initiate conversations with your friends so they know that you are interested in meeting new people—don't take it for granted that they already know that. Friends can see possibilities that make for good connections: a common love of camping, a desire to settle down in the city, the death of a spouse, personalities that would be good together. And, of course, your friends will vouch for you; they may know you better than anyone else. They "pre-qualify" for you.

2. **WORKPLACES**

   Keep in mind that building any kind of a friendship at work can be tricky, but many such relationships become very rewarding. The key is to start slowly, do not jump right into making plans outside of the workplace, and be cognizant of the reporting structure of your workplace. Being friends with your boss, in general, is not a good idea—it really can become a difficult conflict of interests in too many ways. Even more fraught is a boss/subordinate romance, these relationships most often do not end well for either person. Better to stick with peers, or at least those outside your reporting chain.

3. **PUBLIC SPACES: COFFEE SHOPS, BARS, RESTAURANTS, MUSEUMS**

Try going alone, it is the easier way to meet someone, or with a good friend for comfort or safety reasons.

4. **EVENTS: SPORTS, MUSIC FESTIVALS, ART SHOWS, COMMUNITY CENTERS, CULTURAL CLUBS**

   People tend to be happy, celebratory, and friendly at such gatherings, and the setting allows for easy conversation starters.

5. **FAMILY**

   There is sometimes a hesitancy to consider one's family and relatives as a potential source for meeting someone. But why not give it a chance? Tell them the truth: that you are considering new, in-person ways to meet people. Say yes to family parties and celebrations. Attend your cousin's wedding. Commit to helping with the next family reunion. And as with your friends, they too will vouch for you.

6. **VOLUNTEER**

   Almost any organization you might think of would love to have you, so reach out. Any special skills you can offer would be so appreciated.

7. **DOG WALKING/DOG PARKS**

   The proverbial go-to for meeting people. Do you have a friendly dog? Give it a try, even if you don't have a dog.

8. **CLASSES**

   Find a class in a subject that's long been of interest to you, where you are bound to find "like" others.

9. **PROFESSIONAL NETWORKING GROUPS**

   Not just for possible job leads, but to meet people who understand your work.

10. TRAVEL

What state or country have you been wanting to experience? Take a solo trip, or join up with a group.

11. TOASTMASTERS/DEBATE CLUBS

Many ways to increase your talking skills are found here.

12. STANDING IN LINES

A good time to practice smiles and hellos and see where it goes.

13. COMMUTING BY PUBLIC TRANSPORTATION

You must see some of the same people often, anyone you've noticed of interest?

14. PLANES, TRAINS, AND BUSES

People are going places, typically short-lived conversations, good practice.

15. BOOK CLUBS

Few men join book clubs, why not give it a try or start your own?

16. BOOKSTORES

Check out live author readings. Gravitate to the bookshelves that house your interests, maybe you'll find another person there doing the same.

17. HOBBIES

Resume an old one or take on a new one.

18. WORKOUTS

Gyms, exercise classes, dance classes, hiking clubs, biking clubs, etc. These are the types of places where people tend to linger at the end and chat with others casually to get to know each other.

19. GROCERY STORES

Easy to ask a question of someone—
have you ever tried this store's
prepared foods?

20. NEIGHBORS

Get to know the people who live
around you. Say a friendly hello and
take a moment for a little conversation. You never know what you might
learn about them, and vice-versa.
There might be someone right around
the corner they suggest you should
meet. Or maybe you learn that there
is a group that informally gathers at
the park on Saturday mornings.

21. RELIGIOUS GROUPS

Maybe join the chorus or play an
instrument.

22. LEARN SOMETHING NEW

There are so many choices out there: a cooking class, a photography class, a tennis class, a language class, etc. You will need to ask questions and have conversations, it will open you up.

Meeting someone you may develop strong bonds with, and who might become special in your life, could happen anywhere, right across town or in the unlikeliest of places. Whether it is partners or friends that you are seeking, change up how you spend your time and check out some activities and places that you might not ordinarily give a try. Enjoy your adventures!

So we have come to the end. You are now prepared to look up and out beyond your screens, and take in this new, real world idea. I encourage you to enjoy your newfound sense of self, the true you.

GET OUT THERE AND MAKE IT EASY FOR FATE TO FIND YOU. SMILE, SAY HELLO, AND INTRODUCE YOURSELF.

I wish for you friendships and partners, and all the love and romance we each deserve.

Let me know how your journey goes.

You can write to me at:

ashortguidetoahappymarriage@gmail.com

"FOLLOW YOUR BLISS AND DON'T BE AFRAID, AND DOORS WILL OPEN WHERE YOU DIDN'T KNOW THEY WERE GOING TO BE."

—Joseph Campbell, *The Power of Myth* (1991)

Sharon Gilchrest O'Neill, Ed.S.
is a licensed marriage and family therapist and the
author of *A Short Guide to a Happy Marriage*, and
its *Gay Edition*, *A Short Guide to a Happy Divorce*,
Sheltering Thoughts About Loss and Grief, and
*Lur'ning: 147 Inspiring Thoughts for Learning on
the Job*. She has worked both in private practice
and the corporate setting, helping her clients to
examine assumptions, think creatively, and build
upon strengths. O'Neill holds three degrees in
psychology and is often called on as an expert by
a variety of publications, including *The Wall Street
Journal*, *The New York Times*, *The Boston Globe*, and
HuffPost.

About Cider Mill Press
Book Publishers

Good ideas ripen with time. From seed to harvest,
Cider Mill Press brings fine reading, information, and
entertainment together between the covers of its
creatively crafted books. Our Cider Mill bears fruit twice
a year, publishing a new crop of titles each spring and fall.

"Where Good Books Are Ready for Press"

Visit us online at
cidermillpress.com

or write to us at
PO Box 454
12 Spring St.
Kennebunkport, Maine 04046